Food for the Soul

Scripture text taken from The Holy Bible, King James Version.

Poems edited by: Laverne G. Wood
Foreword and Dedication edited by; Georgia W. Allen
Photographs and Art—Hearts and How Can We Hate
By: Wendy L. Jackson

Layout and Design by: Kim Sheffield

To order additional copies of this book, contact:
Xlibris
844-714-8691
www.Xlibris.com
Orders@Xlibris.com

ISBN: Softcover   978-1-4134-8375-8
         EBook   978-1-6641-9392-5

Library of Congress Control Number: 2005900891

Print information available on the last page

Rev. date: 09/09/2021

Food for
the Soul

To the Sweetest Name I Know:
Jesus Christ

IN LOVING MEMORY OF ANEITA JACKSON

This book is dedicated to you Momma—
who taught me to love and give love.

To my father, Mr. Alfair Jackson: It's been a pure pleasure sharing my life with you. Thank you and God Bless You. To my siblings and other family members—I love you.

SPECIAL THANK YOU

To the Rev. Dr. Thomas L. Brown, Sr., Our First Lady, Louise B. Brown, The College Park Christian Methodist Episcopal Church Family, Friends and Colleagues —

To Presiding Elder Albert and Ruenette Lee, III and family.

To Rev. Ronnie E. Brailsford and Rev. Carolyn E. Brailsford and family

To Presiding Elder Jerry D. and Thelma Woodfork

Thank you and God Bless You.

Table of Contents

Foreword

Each day starts with something wonderful. Celebrating life is the first thing that comes to my mind—not just who I am, but knowing that there is a higher power—a higher Being. I know that He is Jesus Christ, my Lord and Savior to whom I give all the praise.

I didn't know that it is in me to express and share with others what God has instilled in me. It has truly been a pleasure to put this book together and to share it with you. May it help to bring love, joy and peace into your lives. The book is dedicated to the Creator, my Lord and Savior. The poems and illustrations are to feed our souls with the love of God. I thank Him that this is all of Him and none of me.

As we travel through life, we often find ourselves planning our own destiny instead of being obedient to God's will and what He has in store for us. I've heard people say, "If I had only waited on the Lord, I know things would be *so much better*." But the flesh often truly gets in the way! This is when we must find it possible to be patient and learn the difference between "head faith" and "heart faith." Know that "head faith" is what our eyes see and "heart faith" is what our heart feels. We must realize that we are all put here for a reason, whether or not we are aware of that reason. The divine plan has already been set, and it is up to us to follow the road to victory.

It is my pleasure to present this book of inspiration to you and, as I have found comfort in doing so, I hope you will find joy in reading it. May the peace of God be with you.

God bless you.

Dreams

Who dares you to dream?
That's what makes the world
go around.

Who dares you to dream?
It's the peace that brings
joy within.

Who dares you to dream?
It's serenity to the soul that
can't be removed.

Who dares you to dream?
It's the whisper in your heart
That tells you to keep on keepin' on.

Who dares you to dream?
It's what life and hope is built on.

Who dares you to dream and tell
You what you cannot do?

So go, and dream your dream.

NUMBERS 12:6
AND HE SAID, HEAR NOW MY WORDS: IF THERE BE A PROPHET AMONG YOU,
I THE LORD WILL MAKE MYSELF KNOWN TO HIM IN A VISION, AND WILL
SPEAK TO HIM IN A DREAM.

11

Hope

Hope is knowing you will always have
Tomorrow

To bring laughter to a child

To offer encouragement to someone hurting

To ask, seek and to give and not to take as we
Often do.

Live life to the fullest for we do not know

Some days will be long and some days will
be short

But as we hope for each new day

Always know there is tomorrow.

GALATIANS 5:5
FOR WE THROUGH THE SPIRIT WAIT FOR THE HOPE OF RIGHTEOUSNESS
BY FAITH.

Life

Who said life was easy; it has its ups and downs

It brings us knowledge and wisdom to help
Us get around

So take the steps along the road and smell
The roses, please

With so much turmoil in this old world,
It's really hard to see

We start out young and then grow old to see what
Each day will bring.

To help someone along the way
My living is not in vain.

To make a difference in each day as we walk
Along this path.

It lets us know while we're on this journey.

That God is the only way!

PSALMS 69:32
THE HUMBLE SHALL SEE THIS, AND BE GLAD: AND YOUR HEART SHALL
LIVE THAT SEEK GOD.

14

15

Hold Out

Help me to hold out until my change
Has come.

Help me to hold out until my victory
Is won.

Help me to hold out until the freedom
Bell has rung.

Help me to hold out until I see the rising
Sun.

Help me to hold out until I make this final
Run.

PSALMS 18:35
YOU HAVE ALSO GIVEN ME THE SHIELD OF YOUR SALVATION;
AND YOUR RIGHT HAND HAS HELD ME UP, AND YOUR
GENTLENESS HAS MADE ME GREAT.

Just Doing Right

Just doing right keeps your conscience clear.

Just doing right brings happiness
To someone's heart.

Just doing right takes fear out of trusting.

Just doing right helps you make it through
Each day.

Just doing right makes you feel right about
Yourself.

Just doing right makes it alright!

19

Time

Take time to know that everything has its season.

Take time to listen when it come to wisdom,
Knowledge and understanding.

Take time to laugh for it brings comfort to the soul.

Take time to live; it's the essence of our day.

Take time to love; it has power to heal the hurt
And sorrow.

Take time to find peace; it's the freedom of our
Spirit.

Take time to share; for it brings hope for tomorrow.

Take time to find joy; it's the goodness of the Lord.

ECCLESIASTES 3:1
TO EVERY THING THERE IS A SEASON, AND A TIME TO EVERY PURPOSE
UNDER THE HEAVEN.

Love

Love may come and love may go.

For we may not know what
Tomorrow will bring.

But always know that God's
Love stays the same.

JEREMIAH 31:3
THE LORD HAS APPEARED OF OLD TO ME, SAYING, YEA, I HAVE LOVED
YOU WITH AN EVERLASTING LOVE: THEREFORE WITH LOVINGKINDNESS,
HAVE I DRAWN YOU.

23

Living in the Spirit

Living in the spirit of what
God's eyes must see.

Living in the spirit of what
People must feel.

Living in the spirit as the hearts
Cry out loud.

Living in the spirit as our minds
Go into our soul.

Living in the spirit as we surrender
All.

PROVERBS 16:19
BETTER IT IS TO BE OF AN HUMBLE SPIRIT WITH THE LOWLY, THAN TO
DIVIDE THE SPOIL WITH PROUD.

Hallelujah

Hallelujah to my soul—this is my song.

It lifts up my heart and brings me joy
I give all praises unto thee.

That's why I sing this song you see
It makes everything okay.

I fall, get weak—and cry some days
and sometimes I cannot find my way.

But I look in my soul to find my song
to help me along the way.

Hallelujah, praise God is my song
I take with me each day!

PSALMS 98:1
O SING TO THE LORD A NEW SONG; FOR HE HAS DONE MARVELOUS
THINGS; HIS RIGHT HAND, AND HIS HOLY ARM, HAS GOTTEN HIM THE
VICTORY.

27

How Can We Hate?

How can we hate when love has no color?

How can we hate when the sun gives warmth and
The moon a calm night?

How can we hate when the birds sing
Melodies on a Spring morning dew?

How can we hate when roses bring sweet
Fragrances on each day that abides?

How can we hate when God gives us mercy and
Salvation?

How can we hate when God is
Love?

People

Some people bring out the best in You
That's what they often say.

Some people make you laugh and cry
And sometimes lose your way.

Some even make you wonder what
Your purpose is in life.

To be a friend or an acquaintance
That remains to be seen.

Just how far they will push that button
To see you go to the extreme.

You are that person in the mirror you
See and of course it starts with you.

That's why some people might just
Bring the best out of you.

DUETERONOMY 7:6
FOR YOU ARE AN HOLY PEOPLE TO THE LORD YOUR GOD: THE LORD YOUR
GOD HAS CHOSEN YOU TO BE A SPECIAL PEOPLE TO HIMSELF, ABOVE ALL
PEOPLE THAT ARE UPON THE FACE OF THE EARTH.

Let Go and Let God

Let go of the anger that's in your mind.

Let go of the hurt that's in your heart.

Let go of the sorrow that fills you with
Pain.

Let go of the sin that's holding you in
Bondage.

Let go of the shame for which you
Have been blamed.

Let go and let God
He'll forgive you for all.

PSALMS 32:8
I WILL INSTRUCT YOU AND TEACH YOU IN THE WAY WHICH YOU SHALL
GO: I WILL GUIDE YOU WITH MY EYE.

33

Loving the Lord

Don't worry about the bills that are due on Friday
Just love the Lord.

Don't worry about how much money you may have in the bank
Just love the Lord.

Don't worry about what clothes to wear each day
Just love the Lord.

Don't worry about what you are going to eat morning,
Noon and night
Just love the Lord.

Don't worry when friends and family turn their backs
On you
Just love the Lord.

Don't worry when your job has stressed you out
Just love the Lord.

Don't worry when people have called you out of your name
Just love the Lord.

When you feel weary and seem like the prayers aren't
Being answered
Just love the Lord.

Remember for all the words that were just said

Know that the Lord will provide and take care
Of all your needs.

Just learn to love the Lord!

PSALMS 107:43
WHO SO IS WISE, AND WILL OBSERVE THESE THINGS, EVEN THEY SHALL
UNDERSTAND THE LOVINGKINDNESS OF THE LORD.

My Prayer of Praise

Dear Heavenly Father—Thank you for this day
That You have blessed me;
Thank You for the love and your annointed
Angels that help me through each day.
Giving praise and honor for all that you do.
Your mercy and salvation that see me through.
The love, peace and joy that you have placed in my
Heart.
Thank you for your bright morning star
That shines upon me, that let's my little
Light shine through,
In Jesus' name, I pray
Amen.

37

Momma

Eggs, grits and bacon for early morning breakfast
That was my Momma.

Working the garden or picking cotton
That was my Momma.

Fried chicken and collard greens fixed for Sunday Dinner
That was my Momma.

Washing clothes or ironing denim jeans
That was my Momma.

Cleaning the house or putting us to bed
That was my Momma.

Helping with homework or telling you it's going to be okay
That was my Momma.

Pressing my hair or cornrowing braids
That was my Momma.

A hug for one a hug for all
That was my Momma.

Singing "Precious Lord Take My Hand"
That was my Momma.

Sparing the rod or going to church
That was my Momma.

Showing you love and how to give love
That was my Momma.

We love you Momma.

(Dedicated to Aneita Jackson)

EPHESIANS 6:2, 3
HONOR YOUR FATHER AND MOTHER: WHICH IS THE FIRST
COMMANDMENT WITH PROMISE; (3) THAT IT MAY BE WELL WITH YOU
AND YOU MAY LIVE LONG ON THE EARTH.

Children

Children running from street to
Street

Are we giving them life or are we
Just cheap?

Just listen, understand, do we really care?

Give them love, joy and happiness

We look the other way when they cry
Out loud.

Some hurting, some mad lashing out
Through the night.

Like a siren on the streets waiting to
Be out of sight.

It's our children that are running; we
must not fight.

For they are our future and our hope
For tomorrow.

PSALMS 127:3
LO, CHILDREN ARE AN HERITAGE OF THE LORD; AND THE FRUIT OF THE
WOMB IS HIS REWARD.

41

God Is

I ask, where is He until joy comes in the morning?

I ask, where is He when the road to victory seems so long
Away?

I ask, where is He when a cool breeze comes on a hot sunny
Day?

I ask, where is He when a rainbow brightens my cloudy day?

I ask, where is He when my world comes tumbling down?

I ask, where is He when I need food for my soul?

I ask, where is He when I feel lost and cold and need to be
Found?

I ask who is He?

He's God.

A friend indeed He is.

EXODUS 3:14
AND GOD SAID TO MO'SES, I AM THAT I AM: AND HE SAID, THUS SHALL
YOU SAY TO THE CHILDREN OF IS'RAEL, I AM HAS SENT ME TO YOU.

Heart

Thank you Lord for letting
My heart feel

For what my eyes do not
See.

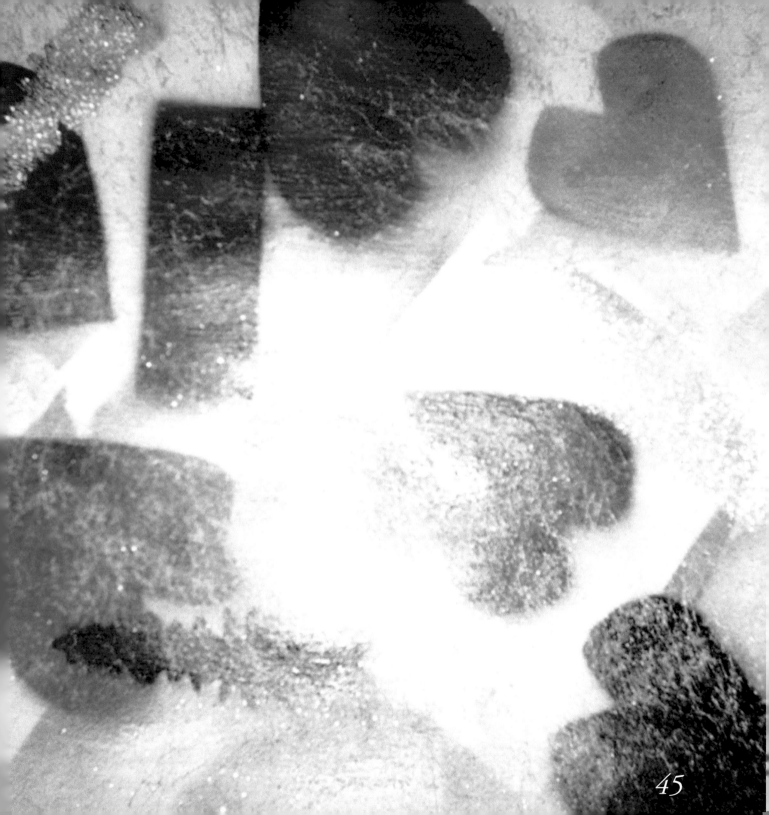

45

Things to Remember

Gold doesn't always glitter.

Money doesn't buy happiness.

Everyone who smiles in your face is not
Your friend.

When you think the grass is greener on the
Other side, you won't miss your water until
The well runs dry.

What's good for the goose is not always
Good for the gander.

Your word is your bond.

First impression is a lasting impression.

A true friend sticks closer than a brother.

Life is sweet, it's what you make of it, But in
This life some rain must fall.

Printed in the United States
by Baker & Taylor Publisher Services